Encyclopædia Britannica

Fascinating Facts

Animals

PUBLICATIONS INTERNATIONAL, LTD.

Encyclopædia Britannica, Inc.
310 South Michigan Ave.
Chicago, IL 60604

Printed and bound in USA.

8 7 6 5 4 3 2

ISBN: 1-56173-316-4

SERIES PICTURE CREDITS:

Academy of Natural Sciences; Allsport U.S.A.;
Animals Animals; Art Resources; Donald Baird;
John Batchelor; Blackhill Institute; Ken Carpenter; Bruce Coleman, Inc.; Culver Pictures; Kent
& Donna Dannen; FPG International; Brian
Franczak; Howard Frank Archives/Personality
Photos, Inc.; Tony Freeman/PhotoEdit; Douglas
Henderson/Museum of the Rockies/Petrified
Forest Museum Association; Carl Hirsch; Blair
C. Howard; International Stock Photography;
Eleanor M. Kish/Canadian Museum of Nature,
Ottawa, Canada; Charles Knight/Field Museum
of Natural History; Vladimir Krb/Tyrell Museum; T. F. Marsh; NASA; Gregory Paul; Paul
Perry/Uniphoto; Christian Rausch/The Image
Works; Peter Von Sholly; SIU/Custom Medical
Stock Photo; Daniel Varner; Bob Walters; Peter
Zallinger/Random House, Inc.

Now That's a Lot of Fish

There are over 30,000 kinds of fish in the world. The largest is the 50-foot (15-m) whale shark and the smallest is the dwarf goby of the Philippines. This tiny fish is less than $^1/_2$ inch (1 cm) in length.

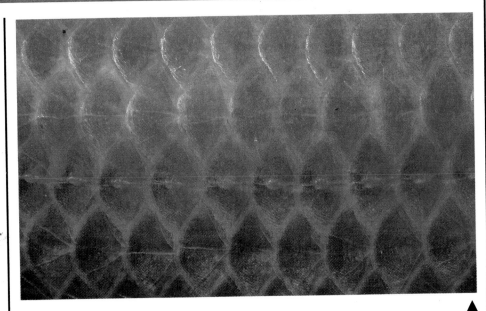

Scaly Creatures

The bodies of most fish are covered with scales. These vary from the teethlike scales of sharks to flat, platelike scales of salmon. In bony fish, scales can be used to determine their age. Usually, scales of bony fish have a fixed arrangement on the body that can be used to identify the species.

Keeping In Balance

Just like in humans, the ear of a fish plays an important part in balance. In the inner ear of a fish, there are three canals that are lined with a sensitive tissue and filled with a fluid. These canals contain ear bones, which are produced from a substance given out by the walls of the canals. They increase in size as a fish grows. At the end of each canal there is a very sensitive swelling. When a fish turns on its side, the ear bones roll and touch the sensitive tissue. A message is sent to the brain—the fish then knows that it is not upright.

A Sense of Taste

Fish have taste buds scattered all over the surface of their bodies. In some fish, they are widely scattered. In others, they are concentrated in the area around their mouths.

The Art of Breathing Underwater

Fish breathe through their gills, which are always found between the fish's mouth and the place where its food goes down. Most of them get oxygen from the water that passes through their gills. Carbon dioxide is then passed out of the gills when the fish breathes out.

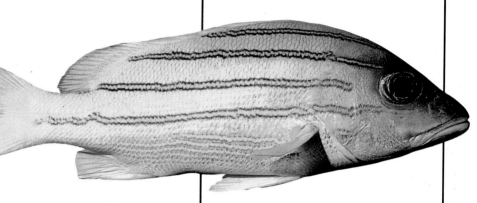

Fish That Build Nests

Some fish are called "bubble nest builders" because of the strange nests they make. The males make these nests by blowing bubbles of air and slime, which they push together to form a mass of foam that floats on top of the water. The female then lays her eggs and puts them in the nest. The male stands guard, catching any eggs that fall out and making sure that they get back into the nest. Gouramis and fighting fish are two of the best-known bubble nest builders.

Friends and Enemies of the Deep

Many fish recognize each other underwater by their colors. Since the bright colors of many fish are in definite patterns, they seem to be able to recognize other fish that have the same colors and markings. These identification marks are also used by fish as a way to hide from their enemies.

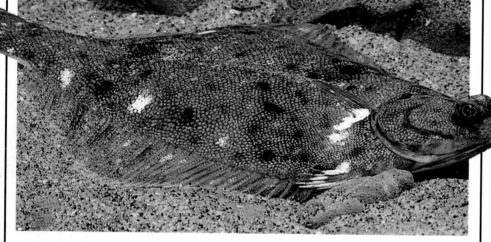

Changing Colors to Suit Fishy Needs ▲

Surprisingly, almost all fish can change their colors to suit their environment. For fish like trout, this can take a long time. Some tropical fish can change from black to white or from bright yellow to scarlet almost instantly. Flatfish like flounder can change colors so successfully that they can be almost impossible to see when they are resting on the bottom of the sea.

Learning Under the Seas

You probably never thought of fish as being very smart or highly developed. The truth is that they can learn. For example, fish memorize smells and colors. This knowledge is especially useful to them when they hunt or when they try to remember where they are going when they travel long distances.

You *Can* Talk on Fishing Trips! ▲

According to most scientists today, it is not very likely that fish can hear, at least not in the same way that we can. However, they are sensitive to vibrations coming through the water, and if a noise is loud enough to make vibrations, the fish are likely to notice it. So, you don't have to keep quiet on a fishing trip—a nice quiet voice is just fine.

Underwater ▲ Kangaroos

Like kangaroos, sea horses have pouches in which they carry their babies around. But, unlike kangaroos, it is the father, not the mother sea horse, who carries the young. In fact, the "daddy" sea horse even carries the eggs around in his pouch until they hatch.

The Biggest Creature of Them All ◄

As far as anyone can tell, not even the largest dinosaurs were as big as the blue whale. Up to 98 (30 m) long and weighing as much as 143 tons (129 metric tons), these giants are really the biggest animals ever to swim or walk on this planet.

Thar She Blows!

When a whale returns to the surface from a dive under the water, it blows the used air out of its body through one or two blow-holes on the top of its head. This used air goes out with so much force that the noise can be heard far away. Since that air is loaded with water vapor, a smoky mist usually comes out of the blow-hole(s) at the same time. Old stories recount that sailors shouted "Thar she blows!" whenever they saw this.

Whales on Land?

▲

Unlike sharks, whales are mammals. They have warm blood, their young are born alive rather than in eggs, and they nurse their young on milk. Strangely enough, it is quite likely that the ancestors of whales did not come from the sea. Inside whale flippers are bones arranged very much the way they are in animal paws. Many scientists believe that whales' ancestors first lived on land and then moved to the sea.

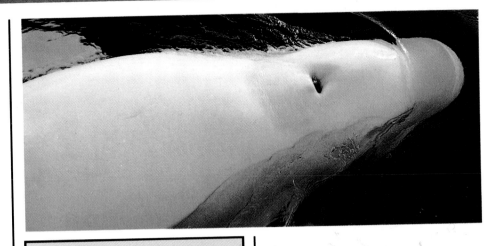

Coming Up for Air ◀

Whales breathe air like land animals; they do not have gills. In fact, they must come to the surface every once in a while to breathe. Whales usually come to the surface every five to ten minutes, even though they have been known to spend as much as an hour at a time beneath the surface.

Eating Like a Whale

Whales usually eat *plankton*, microscopic sea creatures and tiny plants that are eaten by many different sea creatures and small fish. They do not have to hunt down their food. Instead, whales open their giant mouths as they swim through a field of plankton or a school of fish. When the whale shuts its mouth, its meal is trapped inside. All the whale has to do in order to eat is force the water out of its mouth.

Whale-hunting ▶ for Profit

At one time, ships from many countries hunted whales. Their blubber was melted down into oil that was used for lamps. Whalers also took *spermaceti,* a waxy substance that was used in perfumes and makeup, and ambergris, which was also used for perfume.

Protecting Whales from Man

Today, whales are protected by most countries in order to keep them from disappearing from the earth. Five different types of whales cannot be hunted at all, and the International Whaling Commission has set limits on the number of other kinds of whales that can be killed.

Killer Whales Do Attack ▶

Killer whales are the only whales that attack other warm-blooded creatures, and they often eat penguins and seals. They sometimes group together in hunting packs in order to attack other whales and people. Most whales are quite harmless. In fact, most of the famous incidents in which whales attacked ships or boats were the result of people hunting whales.

The Smartest Creature of the Sea

Dolphins are very smart. They can be taught to do complicated tricks at aquarium water shows. In nature, they communicate with one another using a wide range of sounds. At present, scientists are giving them many different kinds of intelligence tests. In fact, there are some people who think that dolphins can even be trained to carry out fairly complicated underwater jobs.

Cousins to Dolphins

Porpoises are closely related to dolphins, but are stockier in shape and smaller in size. They also have blunt noses instead of beaklike ones, and their color and markings are different.

Whales That We All Know

Dolphins are mammals. In fact, they are whales, and they belong to the same family of toothed whales as the giant sperm whales. Dolphins breathe air, give birth to live young, and nurse their young with milk. There are 32 different kinds of dolphins; most live in the sea.

Swimming Like a Porpoise

The strange rolling motion that a school of porpoises makes is caused by their need to return to the surface for air about four times each minute. Their swimming actually takes them up and down as it carries them forward through the water.

On Land and in the Sea ▼

Seals are amazing creatures underwater. Once a seal plunges underwater, its heartbeat drops, so that each lungful of air lasts a long time. Seals can even sleep underwater, coming up to the surface every ten minutes or so for a breath of air. Seals come back to land to breed and to raise their young for their first few days of life.

Those Quick-learning Seals ▲

No one really knows how they do it, but baby seals are able to swim almost from the time they are born. Seals not only swim well along the surface of the water—they are also excellent divers.

Ever-popular Sea Lions

Sea lions are what are known as "eared seals," meaning that their ears stick out from the sides of their heads. ("Earless" seals have ears as well. They simply don't show as much because they don't stick out.)

The Bendable Flippers of Sea Lions ▼

Sea lions can bend their flippers forward, so they can use them to steer as well as paddle themselves along. These bendable flippers also help sea lions scramble over rocks when they come onto land.

Traveling Sea Lions

Sea lions, like many other creatures, migrate back to certain areas when it is time for them to have their young. For example, some sea lions return to the Pribilof Islands, off the coast of Alaska, every May and June to breed and have pups. Then, they take off, spending over half a year swimming around the Pacific Ocean. They manage to travel as far south as California during winter, probably in search of food and warmer water.

Brown Bear Family

Brown bears include the giant Kodiak bear of Alaska and the brownish, yellow-colored grizzly bear of the Rocky Mountains and Canada. Other types of brown bears were once found all over Europe, but have become rare except in remote parts of Eastern Europe.

Just an Ordinary Bear

The black bear is generally thought to be the most common bear in the United States. It is found coast to coast, even in relatively settled areas, where it can be seen sifting through garbage dumps looking for a meal.

Clever as a Fox

Foxes are amazingly cunning and smart. When chased by dogs and fox hunters, for example, a fox will wade across streams to make dogs lose its scent. It will also ride on the backs of sheep in order not to make footprints. Foxes may even pretend to be dead if there is danger nearby.

Foxy Diet

Foxes eat just about everything small enough for them to catch—birds, rabbits, mice, chickens, ducks, and frogs. They will also eat berries, fruit, worms, and bugs.

Shooting Porcupine Quills ▶

A porcupine uses its sharp quills to protect itself. It usually smacks an attacking animal with its strong tail, driving the quills into the animal's face. The quills stick in the enemy and stay there, quite painfully, until the animal can get them out.

Soft as a Baby Porcupine

Porcupines are born with soft quills. Over time, they grow harder and harder, until they become the dangerous weapons that equip fully grown adult porcupines.

Smelly as a Skunk

A Skunk in the House

Before adopting a skunk as a pet, people sometimes have its smelling devices removed by a veterinarian. Unfortunately, without its weapon, a skunk is helpless in the event of an attack by another animal.

Skunks are not unusually brave; it's just that they know that very few animals are willing to attack them. The terrible-smelling liquid that skunks shoot out is so powerful—and so unpleasant—that the only enemy they really have is the owl. Owls can swoop down on them so fast that skunks may not have time to shoot their foul-smelling liquid.

The Story Behind Antlers

Deer lose their antlers every year, and every year they grow back. At first, the new antlers are covered by a hairy skin called "velvet." Once the antlers have grown back to their normal size, the deer begins scraping off the velvet by rubbing the antlers against trees and rocks. In the spring, the deer shed their antlers, and new ones begin growing in their place.

This deer has already lost one antler and will soon lose the other.

Deer with No Antlers

For the most part, only male deer have antlers. Certain types of deer have no antlers at all. The Chinese water deer, for example, doesn't even have tiny stumps on its head. What it does have, though, are two teeth that are longer than the others. These look like tiny tusks as they come out of the deer's mouth and point downward. Another deer without antlers is the musk deer, which makes its home on the lower slopes of the Himalayan Mountains.

America's Common Deer

Two types of deer are common in North and South America. The white-tailed deer is found all the way from Canada to Peru in open woodlands and farming areas. The mule deer lives in mountain and desert areas from Alaska to Mexico.

White-tailed fawn

Antelopes Come in Different Sizes

North American antelopes are generally a little larger than deer. In Africa, antelopes come in all different sizes. The Derby eland, for example, often stands $6^{1}/_2$ feet (2 m) high at the shoulders and weighs 1,500 pounds (700 kg). In contrast, the tiny royal antelope is about the size of a rabbit, not more than 10 inches (25 cm) high, and about $4^{1}/_2$ pounds (2 kg) in weight.

North American antelope

An Elk by Any Other Name... ▲

The wapiti is one of the names given to the North American elk, a giant deerlike animal that once roamed freely all over the continent. Today, it lives mainly in the Rocky Mountains and in southern Canada. It is the second largest member of the deer family. Adult males stand over 5 feet ($1^{1}/_2$ m) tall and weigh up to 650 pounds (295 kg).

Big as a Moose

The moose is the largest member of the deer family. A full-grown bull moose stands about $6^{1}/2$ feet (2 m) high, weighing in at a full 1,800 pounds (820 kg). Its large, leaf-shaped antlers can run 5 feet ($1^{1}/_2$ m) across.

Fierce as a Wolf

Wolves are excellent hunters, and there is little doubt that wild wolves are fierce. The stories about them attacking people are, for the most part, greatly exaggerated. According to most people who study them, wolves attack people only if they have been attacked themselves or if they are extremely hungry. Otherwise, they prefer to be left to their own diet of deer, moose, caribou, and other wild creatures.

Big Cats with a Little Voice

Even though pumas are generally 10 feet (3 m) long, they make a noise almost exactly like that of a housecat—just a little louder. The high-pitched scream that you hear mountain lions making in the movies is a mating call. They rarely use it when they are angry or about to attack.

Wolf Communications

Wolves are extremely intelligent. They are able to live in packs in a highly organized way. They also communicate with each other using a complicated system of barks and calls, facial movements, and body movements. They even use a system of smells to mark off the land claimed by each wolf or wolf pack.

Another Name for a Mountain Lion

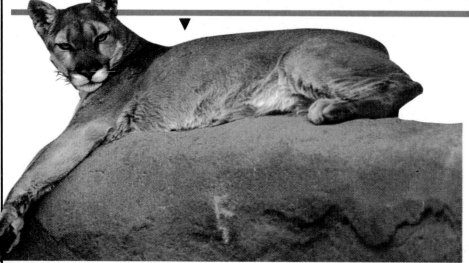

Puma is the real name for the wild catlike creature we sometimes call a mountain lion, panther, or cougar. It is found in North, Central, and even South America, although it is rare in the United States except in Rocky Mountain areas.

The Sharp Eyes of a Lynx

For many years, people believed that the lynx, or bobcat, had the sharpest eyes of any animal. Although scientists are no longer sure that this is true, "lynx-eyed" is still used to describe anyone or anything with extremely good vision.

Prize-winning Hunters of the Night ▲

The lynx is one of the animal world's best hunters. It hunts only at night, when it catches all sorts of birds and small mammals. Lynxes enjoy hunting, and they often seem to break the rule that animals never kill more food than they can eat. In fact, they often get themselves far more food than they could possibly eat, leaving most of a whole sheep or goat behind for other creatures to finish.

A Cat's Largest Relative ▶

The jaguar, America's fiercest and largest cat, is found mostly in the forests and *pampas* (grass-covered plains) of South America. Years ago, jaguars were common in the southern United States and Mexico, but they have become very rare in those areas today.

Spotted Jaguar Coats

Although they are not really closely related, jaguars do look quite a bit like leopards. Jaguars are heavier, shorter, have stronger legs, and larger heads. Most jaguars are golden-brown with black spots. There are jaguars with white coats and black spots as well as extremely rare ones that are almost completely black.

The King of Beasts

◄ For thousands of years, people considered the lion to be the "King of Beasts" because of its strength and fierceness. It is also thought that the lion has a regal manner as it lays watching what is going on around it.

This lion couple has a stately air.

The Many Homes of the Lion

▼ Although we usually think of lions as being one of Africa's most famous animals, they once roamed the plains and forests of Europe and were found as far east as India. In fact, they only disappeared from Europe around the year 500 A.D.

Male and Female Hunters

For many years, people have been told that only female lions hunt. The truth is that both male and female lions hunt. The males are by far the stronger hunters—they can drag an animal the size of a horse quickly to the ground using only the strength of their jaws.

16

Beware of the Lion

Lions are not interested in attacking humans. At times, however, old lions find themselves too slow to attack fast-running antelopes, gazelles, and zebras. Some of them turn their attention to people, who seem far easier to catch. Such cases are rare, and lions have faced far more danger from people than the other way around.

Tigers Are Swimmers▲

Even though we usually think of tigers as animals of the hot jungles of India, many tigers actually live as far north as southern Siberia and northern Korea. They are quite happy living in rocky mountain areas as well as in swamps and forests. They don't particularly enjoy heat, so they tend to hide themselves away in cool, high grass whenever it gets hot. Unlike most cats, tigers are good swimmers. They will often cool themselves off by lying in shallow pools of water.

Tiger Disappearance

Some types of tigers—including the dark-colored tiger off the island of Bali—have already disappeared from the earth. Others, like the South Chinese tiger, are in great danger of extinction. There are probably only 50 to 80 of these creatures left. Scientists fear that of the eight original subspecies of tigers, only three or four will be left by the end of the twentieth century.

The Lonely Life of a Tiger ▲

Except during the mating season, when tigers get together to have their young, they generally live a lonely life. Females have their cubs about once every two or three years, and except for the two years or so when she is raising them, she lives alone. The males also live alone most of the time.

Leopards by Other Names

Leopards are found in many parts of the world, but they are called panthers in both India and Pakistan. There are several kinds of leopards, and they are all excellent hunters.

A Rare and Beautiful Animal

Snow leopards are among the world's rarest and most beautiful animals. They make their home in the Himalaya Mountains, often as high as 18,000 feet (5,500 m) above sea level. Their thick undercoats keep them warm, as do their pale gray outercoats that were once prized as expensive furs.

Disappearing Cheetahs

Today, cheetahs are found mostly in East Africa and Namibia, although a few may survive in northern Iran and Turkestan. They once roamed Africa, Arabia, the Middle East, and the Indian subcontinent. Slowly, they were driven from these lands. In India, the last cheetah was killed in 1948. In Africa, the animals are being driven from the open grasslands they used to live in, as more and more of the land is used for farming and raising cattle.

The Fastest Animal in the World

Exactly which animal is the fastest in the world depends on how you measure it. Cheetahs are certainly the fastest over a short distance; they can reach speeds of up to 60 miles per hour (100 kph) in just a few yards. Over a long distance, most race horses would beat even the swiftest-running cheetah.

The Value of Ivory ◄

Elephant tusks are made of ivory. Ivory is both rare and valuable. The value of ivory has led elephants almost to the point of extinction.

▲ **The All-purpose Trunk**

An elephant's trunk is a very handy instrument, since the elephant can use it as nose, lips, hand, and arm, all in one. The trunk has thousands of muscles in it, and it can bend in just about any way the elephant wants it to. At the end of the trunk is a small "finger" so sensitive that an elephant can use it to pick up something as small as a pin.

Drinking by Squirting ▼

Without their trunks, elephants would find it hard to get a drink of water, since it would be almost impossible for them to bend over far enough to get their mouths into a river, lake, or stream. Instead of lying down completely in order to drink, elephants simply fill their trunks with water and squirt the liquid into their mouths.

Elephants Are Not All the Same

African elephants are different from Asian elephants in several ways. First of all, they are much larger. They also have bigger ears than Asian elephants do. In addition, African elephants have two little fingers at the end of their trunks. Also, both male and female African elephants have tusks; only male Asian elephants have tusks.

Magical Rhino Horns

Rhinos have almost completely disappeared because hunters and poachers slaughter them for their horns. Many people in Asia believe that the horn has magical powers and rhino horn—whole, ground, or even powdered—commands a great price. Hunters will take great risks to kill rhinos and take their horns.

A Very Muddy Bath

Although an entire rhinoceros species has been called "white," they are almost exactly the same color as the more famous "black" rhinoceros. The name probably came about because these rhinos liked to give themselves baths in pools of mud that were light in color.

Rhinos Need Glasses!

Rhinoceroses have a great deal of trouble seeing things that are far away. However, their senses of smell and hearing are excellent.

Move Out of the Way!

Rhinos can be very dangerous. Most keep as far away from people as possible, but once in a while, a bad-tempered rhino will get it into its head to charge just about anything. There is really nothing quite so frightening as the sight of a 10,000-pound (5-metric-ton) rhino charging directly at you.

A Living Dragon ◀

Iguanas are lizards living mostly in North, Central, and South America. Some are small, barely an inch or two (less than a few centimeters) long, while others grow to over 6 feet (2 m). Most of them are green in color, and they look quite a bit like old-fashioned pictures of dragons. Most iguanas live in trees and eat leaves, fruits, and insects.

An Iguana That Swims

The marine iguana lives on the Galapagos Islands off the coast of South America. Unlike other iguanas, it seems quite at home in the water, going there regularly to fetch its favorite food—seaweed.

Leaping Lizards, It Looks Like a Dragon!

Although the Komodo dragon of Indonesia is not really a dragon, it is the world's largest lizard that looks like a dragon. Usually about $11^1/_2$ feet ($3^1/_2$ m) long, it has led to many stories about fire-breathing dragons and monsters. For many years, travelers heard these fascinating stories. In 1912, naturalists were sent to investigate. They brought back stories of lizards growing up to 23 feet (7 m) long. The biggest ones they brought back in the flesh, however, were less than 10 feet (3 m) long.

Lizards Like Meat

Like all monitor lizards (of which it is the most famous and biggest), the Komodo dragon is *carnivorous*—it eats meat. Small mammals, birds, deer, and pigs can all end up as the Komodo dragon's meal.

Bald As An Eagle

◀

The North American bald eagle is not really bald—it just has white feathers on the top of its head that make it look that way. Strangely enough, these birds are not born this way. In fact, it takes them until they are about three years old before their head feathers are white enough to give them this bald appearance.

Electricity Pole Nests ▲

Ospreys are large fishing hawks whose main food is fish, and they make their nests as close to the water as possible. When telephone and electricity poles first came to many outlying areas, ospreys decided these would make wonderful nesting places. Unfortunately, the birds ended up banging into wires, pulling them down, and even putting nests right on top of important electrical equipment. As a result, many of these rare birds were killed and electric power was disrupted often. Rather than fight the birds, electric companies in many areas simply put up empty poles for ospreys to use.

Birds That Like to be Social ▲

Unlike other birds, sea gulls are extremely social. They go around together in flocks, and when it is time for them to breed, they form giant colonies. They also raid people's garbages for food, so they hang out in large numbers around garbage dumps, reservoirs, and even rooftops.

A sea gull waits patiently for its flock.

Vampire Bats Do Feed on Blood

Vampire bats do exist, especially in South America, but they do not turn into human beings, nor do they wear capes and fancy clothes. These tiny bats feed on nothing but blood, which they get by biting animals. They are not a serious problem, since there are not many of them and they live in areas with very few people.

Animals That Fly in the Dark

Bats can fly in the dark because they do not use eyesight when they fly. In fact, experiments show that they can get around just as well blindfolded as with their eyes uncovered. Instead, they use a kind of radar. Bats send out high-pitched sounds that bounce off objects around them. Their sensitive ears are able to pick up the echoes of these sounds—and figure out exactly where things are.

The Changing Diet of Sea Gulls

Gulls were originally hunters. Only in recent years have they learned to eat the leftovers people leave around. In many parts of the world, gulls still hunt fish, shore animals, and crabs. The large, black-backed gull, which may be up to 30 inches (75 cm) long, has even been known to eat mice, lambs, and birds.

The King of Birds

Just as the lion is the "King of Beasts," the eagle is the "King of Birds." Roman soldiers used eagles as symbols of their power, marching into battle behind statues of eagles placed on the tops of poles. Kings and queens of Europe and Asia put eagles on their coats of arms, and many flags and national insignia still show them today. The eagle has even been chosen as the symbol of many air forces.

A Beautiful Feathered Friend

Egrets are large, white birds of the heron family. They were once found almost everywhere in the world. By the 1900s, hunters had just about eliminated them in their greed to get the birds' spectacular white feathers. Most of the egrets surviving today live in Africa.

The Last of the Whooping Crane

The whooping crane, which got its name from the noise that it makes, has almost completely disappeared. It was common right up through the beginning of the 20th century. Hunting and the advance of towns and factories led to its downfall. Now, whooping cranes live in protected areas in Texas. Every year, they fly north to Alberta, Canada, where they nest and have their young.

A Handy Pelican Pouch

A pelican's mouth has a long beak, with a long, thin piece on the top and a large pouch of skin on the bottom. The pouch, which is quite big, can stretch to hold a lot of food. Since pelicans often hunt among schools of fish, they need to catch as many fish as possible. They simply stuff them into their storage pouches and go out and hunt more fish. Then, when they have enough, they sit down and eat.

◄ Talking Birds

Parrots can definitely be trained to talk, although the job is not easy. The most commonly used parrots are the blue-fronted parrot from the Amazon and the African gray parrot. Both parrots make good pets and can be taught to speak in just about any language.

The Life of a Parrot

Parrots mostly get around by climbing. The main use for their great strong beaks is to pull themselves along as they make their way up a tree trunk or branch. Parrots also like to live in groups rather than alone and they make their nests inside holes in trees.

A Bird That Can't Fly

The ostrich is the world's largest bird, but it cannot fly at all. A fully grown male ostrich stands about 8 feet (2.4 m) tall and can weigh as much as 286 pounds (130 kg). It is just too heavy to be taken through the air by its short wings. Ostriches are excellent runners, able to dash along at up to 40 miles per hour (65 kph). They are also good fighters, using their powerful legs to kick their enemies. As they run, they often leap a bit, making it look as if they are trying to fly.

▲ Some Very Old Birds

Cockatoos live a surprisingly long time both in the wild and in the home as pets. In fact, they have been known to live for as long as 100 years.

The Remarkable Cat Family

House cats are really members of the same animal family as fierce big cats. In fact, some of those fierce cats are not much bigger than a good-sized house cat. The bobcat (or lynx) of North America, for example, only grows to about 3 feet (1 m) in length.

Seeing the World Through a Cat's Eyes

Although cats have amazingly good nighttime vision, they cannot see in total darkness. Still, they can see in conditions that would be impossible for you or most four-legged animals. The reason for this is simple. In darkness, a cat's *pupils* (the part of the eye that lets in light) open wide, until they almost fill the eye. This allows any available light to enter, so that a cat can make out what's around it. In brighter light, a cat's pupil narrows.

Man's Best Friend

Bones found in ancient caves and other places show that people have kept dogs for at least 10,000 years—and probably longer. Those dogs weren't pampered pets, though. They were used for work, just like the dogs of American Indians and Eskimos. They were kept to hunt, to guard the family, and to haul things from place to place. Even though they were treated well, their first job was always to help out with whatever work had to be done.

Hamster Happenings

There are many different kinds of hamsters, and a number of them can live as pets or in the wild. The golden hamster—the one you see in pet stores all over—has only been found three times in nature. The first hamsters were not seen until 1830. Then, a hundred years later, a mother and 12 young hamsters were found in Syria. A pair of them were brought to England, where they lived quite happily. Just about all of the hamsters you see today are related to that pair of English hamsters.

A Pig That Isn't a Pig

Even though they share a name, there is nothing connecting barnyard pigs and guinea pigs. They do not even have any connection to the Guinea coast of Africa or the island of New Guinea in the Pacific. The guinea pig is a rodent (just like rats and mice) descended from a family called "cavies." Some guinea pigs still live in the wild in the Andes Mountains of South America.

The Mouse of the World ▶

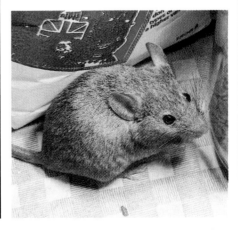

A house mouse is the best-known mouse of all, probably because it is the one people see most often. It lives around people—in homes, offices, and even factories. It is at home in the city or country, in Europe, North America, or Africa. The house mouse originally came from Asia but quickly made its way to just about every place where there are people.

That's a Lot of Cattle

"Cattle" is the term used to describe all *bovines*, which is the scientific name for cows, bulls, steers, buffaloes, bison, yaks, and zebus. "Cow" is the name used for full-grown female cattle; "bull" is the term for full-grown male cattle; "heifers" are young female cattle; and "steers" are males that have been operated on so that they cannot breed.

From the Cow to You

A cow starts giving milk when her first calf is born. That cow will keep giving milk up until just a few weeks before her next calf is born, which is generally somewhere between 250 and 320 days. As long as a cow keeps having calves, it will keep giving milk—skipping only a couple of weeks each year.

More Milk Than You Can Drink

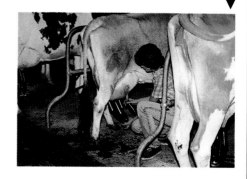

Cows give an amazing amount of milk. During the 250 to 320 days each year in which a cow gives milk, it can give over 4,200 quarts (4,000 liters) of milk. Some cows can more than double this figure, producing up to 9,500 quarts (9,000 liters) of milk each season.

Cows That Give Yellow Milk

Jerseys are the pretty, light-brown cows you see in pictures of all kinds. Although they originally came from the Island of Jersey off the coast of Great Britain, they are now found all over the world. Strangely enough, the milk of Jersey cows is often slightly yellow in color. This yellow color is caused by eating green plants. If Jerseys stop eating greens, the yellow color disappears.

Wonderful Arabians! ▲

Arabian horses are the oldest breed—they have been around for many thousands of years. They have very short backs, small heads, large eyes, and very sensitive nostrils. They usually stand about 15 hands high. Arabians are famous for their lively movements and their great speed. They are also considered the most intelligent of all horses.

The "Hands" of a Horse ▼

It's common to measure a horse in "hands," measurements that are probably based on the width of a person's hand. Each of these "hands" is 4 inches (10 cm). The measurement is taken between the ground and the point at which the horse's neck joins its back.

A Real Beast of Burden ▼

One of the best known and strongest horses that was bred especially for heavy jobs is the Shire horse. Standing over 17 hands high and weighing about 2,000 pounds (1 metric ton), it can pull a load of up to 10,000 pounds (5 metric tons). Belgian and Clydesdale horses are also bred for strength, but they find it hard to match the pulling power of the giant Shire.

Counting a Horse's Teeth

It's easy to figure out a horse's age—just count its teeth. When a horse is between two and three years old, it sheds four middle teeth that are quickly replaced by adult teeth. Another four teeth, right alongside the others, are replaced at the end of the third year. After another year, four new adult teeth appear. After five years, the last baby teeth are shed and the horse has what is called a "full mouth." In most male horses, another four teeth appear. When a horse reaches the age of ten, a special "Galvayne" mark appears, which is a brown groove that runs down each corner front tooth. It remains until the horse reaches the age of 20.

Naming Horses By Color

Horses come in all kinds of colors, although the names used to identify these colors are often confusing. A *bay*, for example, is a brown horse with black legs, mane, and tail. A *chestnut* is reddish-brown all over. *Palominos* are a beautiful gold color, usually with a light or white mane and tail. *Grays* are not really gray at all, but have black and white hairs on black skin. *White* horses are very rare, and most of the horses we call white are simply light-colored ones. True white horses are albinos, and they have red or pink eyes. Another well-known horse, the *roan*, has black, brown, or white hairs sprinkled with white. *Black* horses (the kind ridden by "the bad guys" in Westerns) have to be all black (including their noses, manes, tails, and legs) or else they are called "brown."

Palomino

Children's Favorite Ponies ▲

Shetland ponies are among the best known of all ponies, and they often show up in carnivals and shows, where children are given a chance to ride them. Shetlands are among the smallest of all ponies, usually growing no taller than about nine hands high. Because they are so small, people seem to take an immediate liking to them. Surprisingly, Shetlands are also among the strongest of all ponies. Years ago, they were used inside mines to haul heavy wagons of coal around the underground tunnels.

The Pony and the Horse ▼

There is really not much difference between a horse and a pony except their size, with anything smaller than 14 hands in height called a "pony" and anything larger a "horse." In fact, some horses that are technically ponies by birth are eventually called horses because they are more than 14 hands tall. At the same time, an Arabian is always called a horse, regardless of how tall it is—and it is quite often less than 14 hands tall. If all of this sounds terribly confusing, think of this: The horses used for playing polo are always called ponies—even though they are almost always more than 14 hands high.

Sheep of All Kinds

Even though we are used to seeing the plain white sheep from nursery rhymes like "Mary Had a Little Lamb" and "Little Bo Peep," there are actually hundreds of different kinds of sheep, with wool ranging from pure white to jet black. Some have short wool and others have long, shaggy wool. Even the horns (or lack of horns) differ among the many different kinds of sheep.

Drinking Goat's Milk

People have been drinking goat's milk for thousands of years. It is especially useful for babies and sick people, since goat's milk is much easier for people to digest than cow's milk. In some parts of the world, it is the only kind of animal milk used by people for drinking and for making cheese. Goat's milk is also popular because it causes fewer allergic reactions than cow's milk.

Taking Care of Sheep

Dogs have helped people take care of sheep for thousands of years. In fact, many dog breeds were created specifically to help with this job, since it calls for a dog that is lively, fast, and intelligent.

Unpopular Goats

Goats have been helpful to people for thousands of years and they still have a bad reputation. One reason for this is that the males, called "billy" goats, tend to have bad tempers and an equally unpleasant odor. In addition, goats chew grass and plants right off at the roots. Since they eat so much, they can quickly reduce a lovely field to a barren wasteland. As a result, other animals must move away and soil is washed away.

Useful Goats ▶

Goats provide people with more uses than just about any other animal. They provide milk, meat, leather, and even wool—all without needing a lot of care or feeding from the people who keep them. In some parts of the world, goats are even used as work animals, hauling sleds and carts wherever people need to carry things from place to place.

Getting Wool

Shearing, the process of taking a sheep's wool off, usually takes place in the beginning of the summer when the sheep no longer needs its wool to keep warm. It doesn't hurt the sheep at all, as long as the shearer is careful not to cut or snip the sheep. The hardest part of shearing is cutting off the wool in one big piece, so the wool can be graded, classified, and processed all at once.